THE GRATEFUL DAD'S GUIDE TO THE FIRST YEAR OF FATHERHOOD

How To
Parent Your
Newborn
with Passion,
Joy and
Gratitude

Doug Gertner, Ph.D.
The Grateful Dad

Published by

emu press

Hatching New Ideas Daily
Denver, Colorado

We plant fifteen seedling trees for every 300 Guides printed —
thanks to www.ReplantTrees.org

For more information about how to bring on
The Grateful Dad, contact:
Doug Gertner, Ph.D. / The Grateful Dad
7949 East 28th Place, Denver, CO 80238
303.377.8081 · 303.886.4114
doug@thegratefuldad.org · www.thegratefuldad.org

Dedication

For Maggie
My wife, my partner, my beloved

&

Jordy
My only, my joy, my inspiration

Together you made me
The Grateful Dad

&

For Marc
My first and best teacher

Table of Contents

Acknowledgements

I would like to express my very great appreciation to Chuck Ault, International Training Director, Boot Camp for New Dads, for his introduction to the concept of men-helping-men become great dads, as the facilitator of my very first BCND workshop. His knowledge, skill, experience, kindness and generosity have made all the difference to me and to my work for over 15 years. It was Chuck who first commissioned, directed and edited the original thoughts and monthly advice that became this book. You are a friend who teaches me something new every time we talk, making me think and laugh, while raising the bar and easing the way at every turn.

I would like to offer my special thanks to Haley Ault for her expert proofreading of my first draft. Yes, she's Chuck's daughter, and brilliant, making her the perfect person to read and improve my initial effort.

I am particularly grateful to my friend and guide, Hal Aqua, of Aqua Studio, Denver, Colorado, for the beautiful, professional graphic design, and for tireless work on the original through the final version of this book. As a fellow grateful dad, you made this a labor of love, and your dedication to me and to the project shows up on every page.

Assistance provided by Lisa Maurer was greatly appreciated.

I would like to thank the following grateful dads and moms for reading and reviewing a draft of this book: Brian Elizardi, Mark Nathanson, Ryan Jaret, Jessica DeGroot, and Ken Sanders.

And finally, thanks to all of the grateful dads, moms, and folks who pick up and read this small attempt to make the world a better place through the combination of gratitude and fatherhood.

Introduction: *The Grateful Dad*

To begin, a question.

If I asked you to give me a word or two to describe your father, what would it be? *Kind, generous, distant, absent, reliable, drunk, role model, fun-loving, serious, teacher, happy, sad, provider, hard-working, quiet, intelligent, creative...* the list goes on.

I've posed this very same question to hundreds of men and women over the last 15 years, and their answers paint a picture of our fathers that is both clear and hazy. Dads are good and bad, available and absent, open and closed, active and removed; and fathers are our best teachers about what it takes to be the best possible dad, a grateful dad.

The Grateful Dad?

I myself became a father later than many. Later than my own father who was twenty-seven when I was born. Later than most of my friends who are now becoming empty nesters as I begin to parent a teen. I was thirty-nine when my son was born. Although my wife and partner was, at age thirty-five, considered in medical parlance an "advanced-age pregnancy," there is no similar distinction made for men. Whatever age we become dads seems just right, or at least not particularly noteworthy.

When we decided to become parents, there were obvious roles that could not be shared. But when our son was born, I was intent on walking the talk of involved fatherhood and being a full and active participant in every aspect of his life. I set out to be a truly grateful dad. I changed our son's first diaper and many more after that, and I fed, comforted, and bathed him as often as, and oftentimes along with, his mother. My wife and I both worked full-time outside the home beginning soon after our son's birth, and we each took a half-day off when he needed to stay home sick from daycare. An early indicator of our interchangeability in his life was demonstrated when our young son would call out in the night for comfort using the name "mommydaddy" as a single sort of parent he sought. And as he grows toward being a young man, our connection remains strong, nurtured month-by-month from the time he was born, to this very day.

As The Grateful Dad, I consider my first and most important job to be that of a co-parent to my son. His mom and I both, gratefully, make parenting a priority and work our work-life around family matters whenever possible. I have cultivated a career in speaking and consulting that not only permits me to carve out time to be a full and active father, but also includes a lot of attention to sharing my experience and offering a vision of involved fathering to dads and moms and bosses and employees across the country. The message of The Grateful Dad is simple: be there, be active, be grateful. And if you wonder how to get started down this path, this book is for you.

Be there, be active, be grateful.

How to read this book.

Whether you bought this book yourself, or were given it as a gift from your wife, partner, parents, family, or friends, you'll quickly realize that it is short, sweet and to the point. If your baby is not yet born, you've got the jump on things, and this book is going to help you become a grateful dad from the moment your little boy or girl arrives. And if you're already into the swing of things as a new parent, the month-by-month approach of this little book will make it easy to catch and ride the wave of gratitude, from *delivery* to *delight*. Wherever you are on the journey of parenthood, and whoever you are — dad, mom, grandparent, aunt, uncle, friend, or caregiver — here are some tips for making the most of this small but rich resource:

- **First, read the book cover-to-cover.** No matter where you are in the process — thinking about having a baby, pregnant with one on the way, or already up to your elbows parenting one or more children — get the big picture of how to be a grateful dad by reading through the entire volume from beginning to end.

- **Next, read the book month-by-month.** Again, even if your baby is not brand new, and definitely if she or he is, start at the beginning of the month that corresponds with their age, and read it through. Make mental notes, and notes in the margins, and make sure to discuss it with your partner, and encourage them to read it also.

- **Always make time to take suggested actions.** You'll find that many months offer you specific actions and activities — topics and questions to bring up with mom, or something for you to do or reflect upon. If you are serious about being a grateful dad, be sure to make time to think and talk about and do what's suggested.

- **Know. Try. Remember.** There is additional information at the end of every month telling what you need to *know, try,* and *remember.* Be sure to review and refer back to these points throughout the year.

- **Take *Daddy Steps*.** On page 14 you'll find a model of how every dad moves through year one from *delivery* and *deprivation*, to *discovery* and *delight.* The model assumes that your "Father-Ability," your skills and preparation, increases the more you spend time with your child. This book is designed to increase and support your "Father Comfort," including *Dad Desire* (your motivation), *Dad Ease* (your confidence), and *Daditude* (being grateful every step of the way). Refer back to the *Daddy Steps* model to note where you are in the process. And use the tips each month to get more comfortable as your ability and gratitude increase.

- **Pause and be grateful.** At the end of each monthly section of the book you will find a gratitude journal page. These pages are for you to record specifics of what you're noticing and feeling. You will have the chance to reflect and note your personal gratitude, and what you're grateful for when it comes to mom and baby. Studies show that people who take time to give thanks feel more loving, forgiving, joyful, enthusiastic and optimistic about their futures, while their family and friends report that they seem happier and are more pleasant to be around. Simply making time to be grateful can benefit us in so many ways. That's why I recommend that you note gratitude monthly on these pages.

A final question.

Remember those words that you thought of a few moments ago, the ones to describe *your* father? Well, now let me ask you another question: *When your own child is old enough, and they're asked how they would describe* **you**, *what words would you like them to use for their own father?*

Keep in mind that you are fully and completely in the driver's seat when it comes to what kind of father you will be. Starting right now, at this moment, you can decide who you'll be as a dad, and begin to take the steps and action firmly and confidently in that direction.

Whether your own father was and still is an exemplary role-model for how to be a great, grateful dad, or whether he was angry, abusive, absent actually or emotionally, and even if he died or left when you were very young, he taught you volumes about how to be a father. As you read this book, keep your own father, and other father figures in mind. Take the best of what they did and make it part of your own parenting repertoire, and resolve to do differently those things that you know better as a result of their example. When you are passionate about parenting, with gratitude and extreme commitment, and make every effort to be there physically and emotionally for your child and partner, then you are truly a grateful dad.

Enjoy the book, enjoy the journey.

With gratitude,

Doug Gertner, Ph.D.
The Grateful Dad®
Denver, Colorado
January 2014

Fatherhood: *The First Month*

From Delivery to Delight

Wow! Holy Sh*t! I'm a father. Am I also a Grateful Dad? Soon after delivery of his child, every new father experiences a range of emotions that include excitement, fear, exhaustion, and the feeling of being overwhelmed. Don't worry; every dad is a grateful dad! In the coming pages I'll offer you thoughts, suggestions, and information based on the years of experience I've had and all that I've learned from countless grateful dads. You're not alone — men have been becoming fathers forever — and you have so much to be grateful for.

To begin, check out the model on page 14 that follows how parents and families may develop over the first year. The *Daddy Steps* model begins with *Delivery*, and continues through stages of *Deprivation*, and *Discovery*, finally finding fathers feeling *Delight* in the role of new dad. Please know that while the exact time frame will vary with each family, every new father and mother will likely step through these four phases during the first year or so. Each step takes time and effort...and it all ends in delight. So start at the beginning and keep the end in sight. As an active, grateful dad the best days are all the days ahead.

Every dad is a grateful dad.

The first stage in your Daddy Steps is called *Delivery*, and for fathers this really begins after the birth of your child. With so much time and emphasis put on preparing for labor and delivery, you may not have given much thought to how you will care for your partner as a new mother, and for your new baby after arrival. Even less likely: *have you stopped to reflect on your new identity as a father, and the increased responsibilities this will bring to your own life?*

Daddy Steps Model:
A 12 month plan for being the best Grateful Dad

The *Daddy Steps* model follows parental and family development from delivery to delight. It often correlates with the age of the child, and also aligns with the comfort level of new dads and their motivation to be active and involved in all aspects of caring for their baby. Please note that the time frames for each stage are approximate; every dad will experience these stages at his own rate.

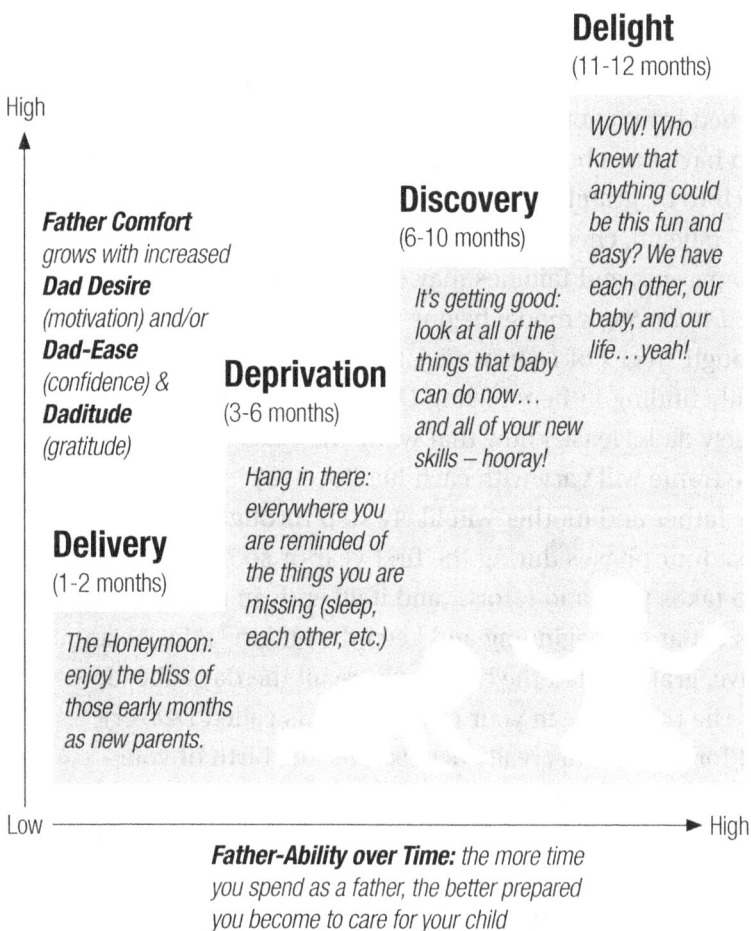

Delight
(11-12 months)

High

WOW! Who knew that anything could be this fun and easy? We have each other, our baby, and our life…yeah!

Discovery
(6-10 months)

It's getting good: look at all of the things that baby can do now… and all of your new skills – hooray!

Father Comfort
grows with increased
Dad Desire
(motivation) and/or
Dad-Ease
(confidence) &
Daditude
(gratitude)

Deprivation
(3-6 months)

Hang in there: everywhere you are reminded of the things you are missing (sleep, each other, etc.)

Delivery
(1-2 months)

The Honeymoon: enjoy the bliss of those early months as new parents.

Low ———————————————————————► High

Father-Ability over Time: *the more time you spend as a father, the better prepared you become to care for your child*

You are still a *man*, yes, and now you are a *father* as well. Are you a grateful dad? Do you celebrate and embrace this new "job" the way you have jumped-in to your other passions in the past? With this new role comes many new expectations. Paramount perhaps to the role of a new dad is to be integrally involved in all aspects of caring for your new baby — right from the start. There is a lot to learn in those first few weeks — how to hold, feed, change, calm, bathe, and dress your baby. This becomes the area where dads bond and the father-child relationship grows. This is also how a mother's confidence is built. When you demonstrate your skills and attitude as a grateful dad, mom will relax and trust you as the full partner and parent you are meant to be. And, in the midst of it all, don't forget that mom needs caring for as well.

While it's true that no parent, or parenting expert, knows everything, it is also a fact that no one knows your baby better than you do. Don't be afraid to ask questions, seek advice, support and assistance, and don't give up. In a very short time — if you remain active and involved — you will master baby care and become a truly grateful dad: the world's greatest expert on your baby.

"If I can do it, so can any other guy who sets his mind to it!"

When I met a grateful-dad-to-be named Brian, one month before his son was born, he told me "I've never even held a baby before, let alone changed a diaper." After delivery, when I saw Brian with ten-week-old Gavin, he told me "I've learned so much since he was born. If I can do it, so can any other guy who sets his mind to it!"

This grateful dad continued: "The first couple days after the birth are just a fog. The nurses took good care of us all — mom, baby, and me. They showed me how to diaper him, and that I could be a big help with breastfeeding. Our first week at home was surreal, too — sleep deprivation does some amazing things to the mind. What I do remember is that we worked as a team, stayed calm and continued to communicate. Looking back, it was a magical time that I'm so grateful to have spent with my wife and our baby."

It's not always easy, and often it can be truly humbling, but with good communication, caring for your new baby will go well and deliver countless rewards.

KNOW THIS:

- **Close-up Viewing.** A newborn can only see clearly objects that are at a distance of eight to ten inches — the distance his face is from yours when you hold and talk to him. So get up-close, look your baby in the eye and talk softly, slowly, often.

- **Goo-Goo, Gaa-Gaa.** A baby's first sounds are not deliberate; rather they are a result of her physical state — being well-fed and content, or in need of something.

- **Spaz!** Newborns have very little control over their bodies. Muscle control starts with the head and moves downward. Sudden, startled movements are normal.

TRY THIS:

- **Keep a journal** of your early experiences as a dad. Record thoughts, feelings, observations, milestones, and the changes you notice in baby every day.

- **Learn your child's cues and signals.** Listen to the sounds she makes, and observe the way she moves, her different facial expressions, and the way she makes eye contact.

- **Respond to your child** quickly, consistently, and predictably. Lots of attention does not spoil babies. Their cries are an important way to communicate. Learn their different cries and what they mean.

REMEMBER THIS:

- **Sleep when they sleep.** Tempting as it may be to try and get a lot of chores and work done while your baby is sleeping, you need to take care of yourself in order to be able to care for them.

- **You are in charge** of who and when visitors come to see your new family. Tell them when they are welcome and what to bring — food, diapers, work gloves.

- **Don't let anyone "rob" you of your newborn.** Everyone will want to hold the baby; you are in charge of who and how long. And be sure they wash hands first to minimize the spread of germs.

Month One: *Gratitude Journal*

Grateful Dad: *What's new, what I notice, what I'm grateful for this month*

_____

_____

_____

_____

_____

_____

Grateful Baby: *What's new, what baby can do, what I'm grateful for with my baby this month*

_____

_____

_____

_____

_____

_____

Grateful Mom: *How are we doing? What can I do for, what I'm grateful to and for my wife/partner this month*

_____

_____

_____

_____

_____

_____

Fatherhood: *The Second Month*

Delivery of a Father

Way to go, you grateful dad! It's your second month of fatherhood and you have truly been delivered. You are making the necessary adjustments and changes to your own life which means, for the most part, you are scheduling your life around the needs of a new baby. For most men, it's very unusual to be spending such vast quantities of time on someone else's needs and activities.

That's exactly what a grateful dad named Juan noted when he checked-in with me at the two-month mark: "Before our delivery, I was not accustomed to thinking about anyone else's needs to such a great degree. But in these first couple of months, my girlfriend and I have gotten into a routine with our baby, and I've found that all of the care the baby needs have become familiar and easier. We've really bonded, too!"

Bonding with your baby begins from the moment you spend time caring for and calming her. When she is awake and alert, your baby observes her world and is clearly aware of you and mom. This awareness deepens the bonding between you and your child, so more time equals greater connection. But it may take some time.

There's so much to do and seldom enough time to get it done.

The experiences of two grateful dads provide a fitting contrast for the varied length of the bonding process. Terrell began by saying "I felt a bond with my baby from the first minute he was born. As soon as I held my child in my arms it was like we'd known each other forever." Then Fabian offered up a very different and funny point of view: "When our daughter was delivered, as soon as her head popped out and her eyes opened, I realized at that moment that she looked *just like my mother-in-law!* Needless to say, our bonding took several months."

To be sure, your awareness increases as you spend more time caring for your baby. Some new dads report that very early on they are able to distinguish the unique cries of their child: to know which cry means "FEED ME!" versus the cry of discomfort from gas or when baby needs a diaper change. These are the very same dads who report a sense of satisfaction and pride in their ability to do what it takes to calm their crying child.

During this second month as a new grateful dad you may be finding that **balance** is an issue, as there's so much to do and seldom enough time to get it done. Whether you both will be returning to work, as is so often necessary in our current economy, and even if one of you is staying home, the teamwork that began in the delivery room must continue in order for all of the baby's needs — and your individual and family obligations — to be met.

Cooperation with your partner and patience with the baby will bring the confidence and balance to sustain you during the early months as parents. While it is true that baby's schedule and needs must supersede your own, have faith, *balance will return to your lives.* And as you await a return to balance, be sure to mark and celebrate the milestones along the way, and enjoy every moment with your baby. You've no doubt had several people tell you, "They grow up so fast." By now you are already recognizing this, so do what you can to appreciate and make the most of every day. Keep a journal.

As one grateful dad put it, "The baby makes my schedule, but my wife and I make the decisions, and *that* makes a difference."

KNOW THIS:

- **BONDING HAPPENS!** Both mothers and fathers can develop a secure sense of attachment with their baby, but they may take different paths to building this sense of closeness and trust.
- **Caregiving = Bonding.** As a new father, you build a relationship through caring for your baby's needs in a consistent manner. Being a grateful dad is an ongoing process. Just do it, every day!
- **Balance takes work.** It's a state of equilibrium that you can achieve, temporarily; and then, just as baby changes over time, your balance shifts, only to be regained again when you make the effort and figure it out.

TRY THIS:

- **Touch, cuddle and show affection.** Touch stimulates the brain to release hormones necessary for growth. Find out how your baby likes to be held.
- **Play with your child.** Simple games can be fun for both babies and grateful dads. Watch to see which games your baby likes and when he is ready to stop playing.
- **Talk, read, and sing with your child.** Babies begin to learn about language from your tone of voice and the sounds you are making, even if they don't yet understand what the words mean.

REMEMBER THIS:

- **Babies Have a Daily Cycle:** A newborn's daily cycle has several states, including:
  > *Actively alert (ready for play and interaction)*
  > *Quiet alert (content to look around)*
  > *Deep sleep (little movement)*
  > *Active sleep (moves around, wakes up if disturbed)*
  > *Drowsiness (transition between sleep and wakefulness, does not respond)*

  Learn to recognize where your baby is in their cycle, and respond accordingly.

Month Two: *Gratitude Journal*

Grateful Dad: *What's new, what I notice, what I'm grateful for this month*

_____

_____

_____

_____

_____

_____

Grateful Baby: *What's new, what baby can do, what I'm grateful for with my baby this month*

_____

_____

_____

_____

_____

_____

Grateful Mom: *How are we doing? What can I do for, what I'm grateful to and for my wife/partner this month*

_____

_____

_____

_____

_____

_____

Fatherhood: *The Third Month*

Dealing with Deprivation

Here's what I often hear from new grateful dads: As you enter the third month with a new baby, your awareness may begin to focus on what's *missing*. The familiar routine of your work and home life before baby has become a fond and distant memory. As your child adjusts to the 'outside world,' you and mom struggle to adjust to the changes this new life has brought to your lives.

With this realization, you have clearly entered the next stage of parental development on the Daddy Steps Model, known as *Deprivation*. You know it's happening when you experience a lack of sleep that begins to catch up with you during a long work day or a middle-of-the-night feeding. You may be getting behind with housework, feeling pressures on the job, and getting concerned if some things have fallen through the cracks.

Your baby needs both parents during this critical period.

Sleep deprivation, which results in fatigue, irritability, lack of focus and a sense of being overwhelmed, makes this a critical time of transition for you as a new dad. Grateful dads who are back at work full-time find that they feel particularly deprived of time with both their baby and their partner, along with missing their old routine — including exercise, friends, media, recreation and more.

The poignant words of a new grateful dad named Dom help remind new fathers that you must reach deep in your reserves during times when you feel most deprived: "I remember that it began to feel like I was drunk, or maybe it was what they mean by an 'out of body experience.' Either way, the result was me not being as sharp as I needed to be, both at home and at work. To get back on track, I looked at what mattered most to me and then began to focus my attention on my wife and our baby, and really using my work time to accomplish my top priorities."

As Dom indicates, an important fact to remember during this time is how much your baby needs you. Several studies have confirmed the benefits to children who are cared for actively by both parents. The different styles and techniques that moms and dads offer their babies serve to complement one another and provide a more complete nurturing that supports their child's ongoing growth and healthy development.

Your baby needs both parents during this critical period, so be sure not to deprive them of your time and attention, even as you attend to yourself, your partner, and your other duties and responsibilities.

KNOW THIS:

- **Grasping.** Your baby may be reaching out to grab toys. Her trust and attachment to you provides the confidence to reach out to discover her environment, an important step in her development.

TRY THIS:

- **Baby Talk.** Hold your baby so that he can see your face. Talk happily to him. Pause to give him a chance to make his own sounds. If he does, repeat his sounds to him. At first your baby may only smile at you. There's a lot for him to learn about "talking."

- **Gimme.** Give your baby different objects to grasp — a metal teaspoon, a wooden block, one of her socks. What is her reaction as she touches each object? Does she prefer one object over the others? Does she look at the object when it is in her hands?

REMEMBER THIS:

- **Play It Safe:** Are your child's playthings safe?

  > Sturdily built so pieces will not break or fall off

  > Have a nontoxic finish

  > No small pieces; can pass the Choke Test (see below)

  > No sharp edges

  > Washable

  > Cords, strings, or ribbons are no longer than 6 inches

  > Toys make gentle sounds rather than sharp, loud, or squeaky ones

  > Cannot be compressed so that the entire object fits in the child's mouth

  > Eyes, noses, and buttons on stuffed dolls are well attached

  > Squeakers are not removable

- **Choke Test:** To see if an object is dangerous because of its size, drop it into a tube 2 1/4" long and 1 1/4" in diameter. (A toilet paper tube is close to this diameter.) If the object fits completely in the tube, it fails the Consumer Product Safety Commission test and should not be used by children under the age of three years old.

Month Three: *Gratitude Journal*

Grateful Dad: *What's new, what I notice, what I'm grateful for this month*

_____

_____

_____

_____

_____

_____

Grateful Baby: *What's new, what baby can do, what I'm grateful for with my baby this month*

_____

_____

_____

_____

_____

_____

Grateful Mom: *How are we doing? What can I do for, what I'm grateful to and for my wife/partner this month*

_____

_____

_____

_____

_____

_____

Fatherhood: *The Fourth Month*

Deprived of Doing It

In month four as a new father, you may be noticing that sleep is only one aspect of what's missing from your typical, pre-baby routine. There has also, most likely, been a change in your intimate, sexual relationship with your partner. Her intense focus on the baby can lead to a reduced focus on you, and this sense of neglect is never easy for a dad or mom.

The first thing to know as you consider this lack of sexual contact since the baby arrived is that it is completely natural and caused by hormones that are tied to the baby's survival. New mothers are biologically predisposed to be preoccupied with their offspring in order to keep focused on protecting the baby from harm. So, if mom seems to want you less, blame it on her biology. Add to this the lack of sleep, and the time pressures you've both been feeling, and it's no wonder there is no time for sexual contact.

Re-think and adjust what intimacy means to you.

Whenever I talk to new grateful dads, the discussion always turns to sex. Like on the reality television show "Survivor," I ask each new grateful dad who feels like he's been voted off the island to respond with YES or NO to the statement: *My sex life has returned to normal.* When the secret ballots are counted, the honest answers are always the same: "NO," we are not back to normal where sexual intimacy is concerned.

While it may come as some relief that your less active sex life is very typical among new grateful dads, what you really need to know is that it will never return to what it was before the baby was born. As one new grateful dad said, "When we were pregnant, people told us 'this is gonna change your life forever.' Where sex with my wife is concerned, that is so true!" He was pleased to learn, however, that research has determined that dads who are highly involved in the daily care of their children actually have more satisfying sex lives than fathers who don't participate actively in such care. It's true! When dad cares for baby, it's a turn-on for mom...and that's always a good thing.

While their pregnancy usually brings couples closer, after the birth many new grateful dads and moms report a swift sense of separation, at least emotionally. You must trust that your relationship will return to some semblance of normal and familiar, at the same time that you look forward to how it will grow, change, and become more intimate and satisfying.

One way to rekindle the intimacy is to re-think and adjust what that means to you. Rather than regarding intimacy simply in terms of sexuality, you can consider how to get close to your partner in ways that are more emotional. Ask about her needs and desires, and tell her what you want from the intimate, sexual side of your relationship. Having these conversations as the baby grows can lead to a stronger relationship, and that will have lasting benefits — not only for you and your partner, but for your child as well.

At this notable time of 'deprivation,' new dads can be grateful to have a partner in parenting, as both of you learn and re-learn together how to be together and enjoy all that you have.

* *

KNOW THIS:

- **Bedtime.** As your baby gets older, he is becoming more alert and active and may have trouble settling down at the end of the day. A bedtime routine may help. A child who can sooth himself to sleep can put himself back to sleep when he wakes up in the middle of the night. And that will let you and mom sleep longer too.

TRY THIS:

- **Bedtime Ritual.** Instead of letting your baby fall asleep while feeding or rocking him, put him to bed while he is still awake so he will learn to fall asleep on his own. Sing the same song or say a certain prayer each time you put the baby down. A key to establishing good sleep habits is getting children to fall asleep on their own — to become self-soothers.
- **Mirror, Mirror.** Though your baby will enjoy and understand mirrors more in a few months, it is not too early to introduce her to some mirror games. Holding your baby in your arms, stand in front of a mirror. Make faces, touch the mirror, and talk about what you and your baby see. Play a game of peek-a-boo by stepping to the side of the mirror.

REMEMBER THIS:

- **You will have sex again:** Some things you can do to make it happen—
  > *Try to spend some time together each day — while the baby's sleeping or safely occupied in a swing or bouncy chair — to check in with your partner and pay attention to her needs and those of the relationship.*
  > *Plan ahead and go out on regular dates; hire a sitter in advance, and go out for a short evening…even if you don't really have the energy or desire to do so. It's vital to your relationship to learn early how to get away and enjoy time with your partner or you'll wake up one day to find it's been years since you've been out together.*
  > *Most couples will experience some tension and conflict in the first few months after the birth. Even those parents who communicated very well before the baby came will find that the added stress of their new responsibilities can create strain. Be kind to your partner, and if necessary, don't hesitate to seek support and counseling from those who might be able to help.*

Month Four: *Gratitude Journal*

Grateful Dad: *What's new, what I notice, what I'm grateful for this month*

_____

_____

_____

_____

_____

_____

Grateful Baby: *What's new, what baby can do, what I'm grateful for with my baby this month*

_____

_____

_____

_____

_____

_____

Grateful Mom: *How are we doing? What can I do for, what I'm grateful to and for my wife/partner this month*

_____

_____

_____

_____

_____

_____

Fatherhood: *The Fifth Month*

Deprivation Blues

With five months of experience as a new grateful dad, you may feel ready to write a book about fatherhood. Then again, when would you find the time? After all, you've hardly had enough time to spend on your top priorities, your family and your job.

I often hear from new fathers, who are truly involved in caring for their babies, that what has suffered most is finding ways to pursue their favorite pastimes. The sports, games, hobbies, and activities, and — of course — the friends they enjoyed before the baby came, are now feeling more like distant memories. Your active role as a *father* seems to have supplanted your well-rounded life as a *person*.

This was certainly my fear, and my early experience as a new grateful dad. So when the *deprivation blues* first hit, here's what I did: I began by making a list of my favorite activities that included *cycling, skiing, travel, hearing live music, and seeing movies.* Next I sat down with my partner, *The Grateful Mom,* and we brainstormed how to bring those back into our life. Slowly but surely over our first year as parents, we were able to re-incorporate many of our favorite pastimes so that our sense of deprivation diminished noticeably.

Deprivation depends on how you look at it.

For example, we bought a used bicycle trailer from some friends whose children had outgrown it and continued to ride our bikes with junior in tow. During the winter months we utilized some of the licensed infant care available at our favorite ski areas, and sometimes we took turns skiing solo while the other person hung out in the lodge with our son.

We also found car and plane travel with a baby pretty easy during the first year, as our infant seat buckled into the airplane seats, and we made certain to feed the baby during take-off and landing to prevent the pressure changes from hurting his ears. Another time, during a road trip, we were pulled over for driving too fast through a small town speed trap. When approached by the officer, who also happened to be a father, our baby began crying as if on cue, and we were sent on our way with a mix of pity and empathy...*and no speeding ticket.*

We continued to enjoy some of our other, pre-baby pastimes, although with some distinct modifications. For instance, our movie viewing was more often accomplished on pay-per-view and DVD, thanks to Netflix and our investment in a home theater system. Some other parents we know like to take turns going out to first-run films — she'll go to the early show, then he will duck out for a late screening. After both parents have seen the picture, they compare notes as if they had attended the movie together.

As for concert-going — while we certainly spend less time hearing our favorite bands at big arenas, or keeping up with new music at smaller clubs, it's been easy to enjoy lots of recorded live music thanks to a steady supply of concert CDs that I buy, burn, or trade with friends. Whole shows are available to stream, and concert videos are a favorite as well.

For me anyway, deprivation depends on how I look at it. Being a father continues to be just plain fun, and many new grateful dads have realized, as I did, that while you really don't need to leave behind old pastimes, having children also means we have a great, *new hobby* to enjoy. Bring on the discovery!

KNOW THIS:

- **You Cannot Spoil a Baby.** You may begin to think that you should change the way you respond to your baby so that he does not become spoiled — for example, to delay going to him when he cries. The truth is, it will be less work and less stress if you meet his needs without unnecessary delays. It is easier to feed, diaper, and play with a baby who is not overly stressed, tired or anxious from excessive crying. Delays can make your baby more demanding, and he may lose trust in his ability to get his needs met. For now, your love and attention are what he needs.

TRY THIS:

- **Rolling Over.** At this age, your baby may be getting ready to roll over from his back to his stomach. To see how close he is to accomplishing this feat, lay him on his back and get his attention by showing him a toy. Move the toy to the side and top of his field of vision. You want him to turn his head and shoulders and arch his neck and back.
- **Laughing.** A baby first laughs at around four to five months of age. Kisses on her tummy will bring on a squeal of delight. At this age, your baby's laughter is probably a reaction to something that feels good or is physically exciting.

REMEMBER THIS:

- **Your life will be full and varied again:** Right now the baby is your primary focus. To move toward balance and back in the direction of your other favorite activities, use the chart below and note the following:
  - > *ACTIVITY — list all your favorite things to do before the baby came*
  - > *PRIORITY — rank each activity according to preference/importance to you*
  - > *FREQUENCY-current/desired — how often do you now and do you want to do this?*
  - > *STRATEGY — what can and will you do to move toward getting back to this activity?*
  - > *ALTERNATIVES — what could you do to get a similar experience if it is not possible to do the activity the same as before baby?*

Activity	Priority	Frequency	Strategy	Alternatives
Example: Workout @ gym	1	Current: 0 times/week Desired: 3 times/week	Go to gym on lunch hour twice/week + to gym on one weekend day	Workout @ home: get basic gear and set a time to use it every other day

Month Five: *Gratitude Journal*

Grateful Dad: *What's new, what I notice, what I'm grateful for this month*

_____

_____

_____

_____

_____

_____

Grateful Baby: *What's new, what baby can do, what I'm grateful for with my baby this month*

_____

_____

_____

_____

_____

_____

Grateful Mom: *How are we doing? What can I do for, what I'm grateful to and for my wife/partner this month*

_____

_____

_____

_____

_____

_____

Fatherhood: *The Sixth Month*

Dad's Discovery

At about six months, the *Discovery* phase begins and fatherhood truly starts to get fun. Many dads describe this as the time when they know that bonding is in full-swing. "She smiles at me, and really reacts when I walk into the room," says Kahlil of his daughter Lena. "Every day she does something new, and my wife and I are on a steep learning curve to keep up with our baby's many changes." If this sounds familiar, then you are also probably feeling more confident and satisfied as a grateful dad, even as you are facing new changes and challenges daily as a parent.

With all of these changes in your baby and your life, this is also a time when you may be discovering some tension with your partner. Now is the time to explore variations in your "routine" that permit more flexible scheduling for both of you. Are you spending time doing what you want and need for family and work? Does each of you feel that responsibilities are divided fairly and shared equitably? Do some things need to be re-thought or rearranged in order for better balance to be attained? Start by discussing your individual needs, and continue the discovery process to determine how to best work together so that everyone — you, mom, and the baby — gets what they are seeking.

"She smiles at me, and really reacts when I walk into the room."

Throughout this process of learning, changing, and growing together as a family, keep in mind that you and your partner grew up in distinctly different families. These different *families of origin* mean that you are each using a unique *road map* to navigate your journey through early parenthood. Many couples realize their early experiences within a family — the differences between their own parents, and the number or age ranges of siblings — have a direct effect on how each approaches being a parent. Keep in mind amidst the frustrations you may encounter on this path, that *both* of you have valuable and necessary experiences and insights to share. An extra effort of kindness and flexibility guides new grateful dads and moms at this crossroad.

At this stage, baby is undergoing some major physical changes. Has your pediatrician suggested the introduction of solid food to the baby's diet? This new eating option — and a new tooth — often happens around age six months. Be aware that once your baby starts on solids, such as rice or wheat cereal, you are in for a new 'discovery' every time you change a diaper. As one grateful dad put it, "When my daughter was breastfeeding, her poop didn't seem to smell bad at all, but that all changed when we got the go-ahead to feed her real food. Whoa! Now I can smell her from the next room and I definitely know when her diaper needs changing."

With so many new things to discover, grateful dads are like explorers of uncharted territories. Happy hunting, and enjoy all that you find!

• •

KNOW THIS:

- **Drowning.** Never leave your baby alone in a bath or near a pool of water, no matter how shallow it is. Babies can drown in just a few inches of water.

- **Going Solid.** Introducing solid foods is best done on the advice of your pediatrician, and it does not signal the end of breastfeeding. Breast milk is recommended for the first year, if possible; it's helpful in keeping baby healthy. Solid foods — cereals, vegetables, fruits, etc. — are added slowly. Let baby be the guide.

TRY THIS:

- **Straight Talk.** You've been parents for half-a-year now; it's time to take stock. Make time to discuss some of these questions:
  > *Are we each spending time doing what we want and need for ourselves, our family, and our work? What adjustments might we consider?*
  > *Do we each feel that responsibilities are divided fairly and shared equitably? Housework? Childcare? Earning?*
  > *Do some things need to be re-thought or rearranged in order for better balance to be attained? Where do we start?*

REMEMBER THIS:

- **Our family of origin provides the road map we most often travel as new parents:** To chart your own paths as a grateful dad and mom, consider —
  > *What are my earliest memories of my parents? Faint, fond, familiar?*
  > *What did I learn about parenting from my own parents, by words and deeds? What did they say explicitly and by example?*
  > *How do my birth order and sibling relationships show up in my expectations and approach to being a parent?*
  > *In what ways do my early family experiences differ from that of my partner? How are our families similar? Does this make it easier or more difficult for us to parent together?*
  > *What are the best attributes and qualities that I can bring from my family of origin into my own new, nuclear family.*
  > *What will I do differently as a parent, based on my own awareness and reflection about my family of origin?*

Month Six: *Gratitude Journal*

Grateful Dad: *What's new, what I notice, what I'm grateful for this month*

_____

_____

_____

_____

_____

_____

Grateful Baby: *What's new, what baby can do, what I'm grateful for with my baby this month*

_____

_____

_____

_____

_____

_____

Grateful Mom: *How are we doing? What can I do for, what I'm grateful to and for my wife/partner this month*

_____

_____

_____

_____

_____

_____

Fatherhood: *The Seventh Month*

Discovering Balance

By month seven you have discovered the many challenges of balancing your new role as a father with your ongoing role as husband or partner and the ever-present responsibilities of your work. Take a moment to reflect, and *applaud yourself* in appreciation for all that you are accomplishing. As one grateful dad put it "I bring home the bacon and fry it up, bathe my baby — and sometimes my wife — and I usually end up doing the dishes and balancing the checkbook too."

If this sounds familiar to you, then you are starting to sound like *superman* to me. It reminds me of something my friend Dr. Bob Brannon, a psychologist and author, once wrote about the four main messages that men get during our lives. Over and over, according to Brannon, men are told: *No Sissy Stuff* — don't act like a girl or a woman, and don't be open or vulnerable; *Be the Big Wheel* — gain status, achieve success, and strive to be looked up to by others; *Be the Sturdy Oak* — have an air of confidence and toughness, and always be self-reliant; and *Give 'Em Hell* — men have an aura of aggression, daring, and violence.

If you recognize these expectations, then you've truly been raised as a typical male in Western culture. Unfortunately, these familiar aspects of the male role sometimes lead fathers to withdrawing — emotionally, physically, or both — and leaving baby care, housework, and nurturing to others. While sometimes this path seems easiest or necessary to a father, there is much evidence to discourage this all too typical and often tragic option.

Several studies over the last twenty-five years have pointed to the vital role that fathers play in the healthy, positive development of their children. To begin with, infants who have time alone with their dad show richer social and exploratory behavior than children who are not exposed to such experiences. Father involvement is the strongest parent-related predictor in the development of empathy in a child, and it is also closely associated with learning effective problem-solving skills. Research has also repeatedly shown that involved dads help their children do better in school and stay out of trouble with the law. If that's not enough data to convince dads to be active with their kids, just let me know and I'll cite several more studies to make the important case for being a grateful dad and staying involved emotionally and physically in the life of your child.

Travel together through the precarious path of balanced parenting.

It seems quite clear that the best option is for both parents to stay the course and travel together through the precarious path of balanced parenting. Be patient with each other as you continue to marvel at how your baby is developing, and collaborate to discover the skills and perseverance to manage each challenge you encounter.

• •

KNOW THIS:

• **Separation.** At about this age your baby may begin to discover that Mom and Dad are separate people from himself and that you are his favorite people to have around. At the same time, he does not clearly understand that you still exist, even when he cannot see you. Gradually, through experience, your baby will learn that when you go away, you do come back.

TRY THIS:

- **Separation Without Anxiety.** To help your baby handle anxiety about leaving:

  > *Develop a predictable routine that you go through whenever you leave. Practice your routine even when you go to another room for a brief time — "Bye, Bye. I'll be back... Here I am again (accompanied by a hug or touch)."*

  > *Say your goodbyes and then leave. Lingering and waiting for your baby to calm herself can prolong the suffering. After you leave, she can more easily be redirected.*

  > *Always tell your child you are leaving and that you will be back. Sneaking away will make him more watchful and feeling that he needs to keep an eye on you because he cannot trust that you will not leave.*

  > *Accepting that your child's anxiety is real and normal for her stage of development can make it easier for you to live with her need to be within sight of you. Ignoring her feelings will only make her more anxious.*

  > *Give your baby time to check out new people.*

REMEMBER THIS:

- **No Man is an Island.** Ask yourself: How do I accept, buy-in and behave according to these typical male messages? How am I (or do I want to be) different?

  > *No Sissy Stuff — don't act like a girl or a woman, and don't be open or vulnerable;*

  > *Be the Big Wheel — gain status, achieve success, and strive to be looked up to by others;*

  > *Be the Sturdy Oak — have an air of confidence and toughness, and always be self-reliant; and*

  > *Give 'Em Hell — men have an aura of aggression, daring, and violence.*

Month Seven: *Gratitude Journal*

Grateful Dad: *What's new, what I notice, what I'm grateful for this month*

_____

_____

_____

_____

_____

_____

Grateful Baby: *What's new, what baby can do, what I'm grateful for with my baby this month*

_____

_____

_____

_____

_____

Grateful Mom: *How are we doing? What can I do for, what I'm grateful to and for my wife/partner this month*

_____

_____

_____

_____

_____

_____

Fatherhood: *The Eighth Month*

Dad is Discovered

Around eight months, new dads make an amazing discovery: "she notices me!" No, I don't mean your wife; I'm talking about your baby. Although she has actually known your voice, touch, and smell all along, now your baby begins to show signs of recognition and eagerness when you are around.

A new grateful dad named Dave marveled at the recent changes in his son: "When I walk in the room, Bergen starts to kick his feet and wiggle his body. When our eyes meet, his smile is as wide as mine." The rewards of fatherhood are summed up on the faces of our new babies. If that doesn't make you a grateful dad, I don't know what will.

> *"When our eyes meet, his smile is as wide as mine."*

And, in turn, fatherhood is its own reward as your confidence grows with the discovery of how much you know about your child. You are familiar with the meaning of her cries, and can interpret and respond to gestures and facial expressions. Remember, the more time you spend active and involved with your baby, the more you will learn and the better life will be for all concerned.

For some babies, eight months is also the beginning of a true milestone in their discovery process: crawling. As your baby gets more mobile, you will need to make accommodations to both her physical environment and to your approach to parenting.

Mobility means it's time to take a good look at the furniture in every room and assess the safety hazards wherever baby may go. There are many resources to guide your new task of *baby proofing*, and the goal from now on is to stay one step ahead, literally, in order to keep baby safe.

The advent of crawling will also call for some discussion with your partner about how comfortable each of you is with your baby's *seek and discover* missions. Research says that, as a dad, you will likely be more inclined to let the baby travel farther and explore more widely than mom is. Before any tension develops over how much to let your child discover on her own, be sure to talk with mom and agree how you want to handle this combination of newfound mobility and boundless curiosity.

You have also no doubt discovered just how long it takes to get anywhere with the baby. Although it may seem like spontaneity is a thing of the past, a bit of planning and flexibility can still permit your family to have some great adventures. One grateful dad shared these thoughts and recommendations: "We keep a fully stocked diaper bag, packed and ready, by the front door. Mine is a nice backpack with everything the baby could need when we are away from home. We have an umbrella stroller in both cars at all times, and our cellphones handy to stay in touch with each other and if we need to call ahead to our destination."

As a rule, dads report that they discover great satisfaction in meeting the daily challenges of fatherhood. So, venture forth with baby and with gratitude. Dads Rule!

KNOW THIS:

- **Talk Talk.** Your child's language development depends on physical growth, cognitive development, and his hearing. An infant whose hearing is developing normally can respond to different tones of voices and distinguish between voices. As he gains control of his lips, jaw, tongue, and vocal cords, he can begin to babble. Gradually his babbling turns into sounds that are more like adult speech patterns, though words do not come until his first birthday or later.

TRY THIS:

- **Giving Voice to your Baby.** How to help your child to listen and to talk…
  - > *Give uninterrupted one-to-one conversation time with your child.*
  - > *Use your child's name often as you talk to her.*
  - > *Your child will first learn the names of things. Say, "Where did your ball go?" rather than "Where is it?"*
  - > *Talk about things that are physically present so your child can make the connection between the word and the object. Point to things you are talking about.*
  - > *Talk about things that interest your child — things you have done together, his toys, what he eats…*
  - > *Be enthusiastic and expressive in your speech.*
  - > *To encourage her efforts at speech, do your best to understand her gestures, words, or invented words.*
  - > *Talk to your child in a comforting voice. Harsh sounds may make him afraid and limit his interaction.*
  - > *Talk about what you are doing. Use routine care times to talk to your child.*
  - > *Sing songs and say rhymes to your child.*
  - > *Repeat the sounds that your child says to you. Make a game of it.*
  - > *Look at books and talk about the pictures. Ask your child to point to pictures in the book, "Where is the truck?"*
  - > *Play music — all kinds of music (but not too loud). Make up songs. Dance to the music.*

REMEMBER THIS:

- **Playing it Safe.** As your baby becomes more mobile, it is important to keep one step ahead of his abilities. Look at your home from your child's perspective — what looks interesting, how high he can reach, how well and how far he can travel, and what new skills he is acquiring. Check the following:
- HOME FURNISHINGS
  - > *Be sure furniture is sturdy enough for child to use to pull herself up*
  - > *Keep electrical wall sockets covered*

> *Put gates at the top and bottom of the stairs*
> *Cover sharp edges and corners of furniture*
> *Secure or put barriers in front of plate glass windows, windows with flimsy screens, patio doors, and balcony windows*
> *Keep things that dangle out of reach or tied up — drapery/blind draw cords, table lamp/appliance cords, tablecloths*

- BURNS
  > *Keep radiators, fireplaces, and space heaters out of reach*
  > *Set the water heater no higher than 120 degrees*
  > *Keep hot foods and drinks on the stove's back burners and away from table edges*
  > *In the bathtub, turn your child away from the faucet*

- POISONS
  > *Keep cleaning and gardening supplies, medicines, and beauty products in locked cabinets*
  > *Remove or protect from lead paint*
  > *Keep poisonous plants out of reach*

- SUFFOCATION
  > *Keep plastic bags out of reach*
  > *Don't allow your child to play with anything small enough to be swallowed*
  > *Keep balloons out of reach; popped/uninflated balloons are choke hazards*
  > *Cut food into small pieces; cut round foods (grapes, hot dogs, bananas) into irregular pieces*

- OTHER TIPS
  > *Keep plastic bags out of reach*
  > *Be wary of places into which your child can get in but not out*
  > *Watch your child around pets — dogs, cats, hamsters, fish...*
  > *Keep guns unloaded and locked up; lock ammunition in a separate cupboard*
  > *Install smoke detectors in each bedroom and on every level; put a CO_2 monitor on every floor of the home*

Month Eight: *Gratitude Journal*

Grateful Dad: *What's new, what I notice, what I'm grateful for this month*

_____

_____

_____

_____

_____

_____

Grateful Baby: *What's new, what baby can do, what I'm grateful for with my baby this month*

_____

_____

_____

_____

_____

_____

Grateful Mom: *How are we doing? What can I do for, what I'm grateful to and for my wife/partner this month*

_____

_____

_____

_____

_____

_____

Fatherhood: *The Ninth Month*

An Odyssey of Historic Discovery

As you arrive at the ninth month of fatherhood, you and your partner are discovering which roles and routines work best for providing babycare and maintaining family balance. The goal of equal time spent with your baby may have morphed into some patterns that look more like traditional gender roles. Now may be a good opportunity to spend some time discussing with mom how these roles are working for each of you. It is important to note which tasks you and she typically take responsibility for, which of these duties you each find most satisfying, and which seem more mundane. As you continue to develop your parenting team, consider who does what and if these arrangements are best for each of you and for the baby.

With new doors opening came a range of new roles.

At this time it may be helpful to understand how the role of a father has evolved over time. Scholar and author Dr. Joseph Pleck traced the history of fatherhood in America for the last 300 years and discovered just how much it has changed. According to Pleck, the Victorian father was "Moral Overseer" of his family — the one who taught them right from wrong, good from bad, and to fear God. This is a noble and necessary role for a father, to be sure, yet Pleck notes that fathers in this era showed little affection to their children, especially sons.

During the mid-19th to early 20th centuries, after the industrial revolution, the role of fathers became that of "Distant Breadwinners." For the first time, a father's work was sited away from their immediate home; where once dad ventured only as far as the fields out back, or his blacksmith shop next door, now he left for factories and offices, perhaps hours away. In this period, domestic duties most often fell to mothers, and although fathers maintained responsibility for moral teaching and discipline of their families, it was moms who cared for kids and managed the household. Thus it was probably during this era that mothers first uttered those immortal words *"Wait until your father gets home!"*

Wartime in America saw fathers leave home in great numbers to defend their country — Distant Breadwinners, still — and when they returned, after World War II and through the Mid-1960s, they became what Pleck calls "Sex-Role Models," seeking to show men, women, and children the 'proper' way for each gender to behave. These Sex-Role Models defined and demonstrated their expectations of how masculinity and femininity should look in post-war America, and in so doing, they stayed aligned with the narrow stereotypes of traditional gender roles.

With the 1970s, 80s, and 90s came the so-called "New Father," a mix of all the old roles combined with new norms and opportunities spawned by the Women's Movement and fueled by a tighter economy. These dads were the first to attend and participate in the births of their children, to actively share in the care of their infants, and to engage equally in the lives of their daughters as well as sons. With new doors opening came a range of new roles, and no small measure of confusion for these more involved New Fathers of the 70s, 80s and 90s.

That brings us to the present: a time I call "Dawn of the Grateful Dad: A Fatherhood Odyssey." With the emergence of new fatherhood movements, such as Boot Camp for New Dads, there are new opportunities to balance our traditional roles and our work with the joys of co-parenting and full and active involvement with our children and partners. And while all of the previous roles are still present among fathers, and each of these types of fathers certainly has a positive aspect to it, the grateful dad of the future (that's you!) will chart new territory to create a unique version of his important role that is at once informed by the past and fully in step with the present needs of himself and his family. As they say, "the more things change, the more they stay the same." Enjoy your odyssey!

KNOW THIS:

- **Competence.** Since her birth, your child has become more skilled at living in the world. She will continue to develop competence in developing relationships with others, controlling her body, and knowing about the world and how things work. Young children are very curious. It is their nature to want to explore everything — things in which adults often have no interest. Your child may explore dust balls to know how they feel, corn husks to know how they taste, or the sound of pans banging on the floor.

TRY THIS:

- **Social, Mental, Physical Competence.** As a parent, you will want to encourage this curiosity and your child's mastery of various worlds.
  > *When your child tries to communicate with you through gestures or body posture, acknowledge his attempts by trying to understand them and responding to them.*
  > *Provide opportunities for your child to play with other children.*
  > *Help your child practice separating from you and work toward allowing strangers to care for her.*
  > *Talk with your child about what she sees, what you are doing, and how things work. As she learns to talk, ask questions of her.*
  > *Provide opportunities for your child to do things for himself or for you to provide only partial help — feeding himself, taking off socks, washing his tummy...*
  > *Provide a safe environment where your child can freely explore.*
  > *Put toys on low shelves so your child can select the toy he wants to*

play with. If it is safe, be accepting of what your child likes to explore and be tolerant of temporary messes and clutter.

> *Allow your child to struggle. The feeling of "having done it myself " is a great booster of one's self esteem. Intervene if he becomes frustrated or before he gives up because the task is too difficult.*

> *While watching or playing with your child, notice what she can do and try to think of materials or games that might extend her learning or development of skills.*

REMEMBER THIS:

- **Fathers Have History.** Ask yourself: How am I similar to other fathers throughout history? What about my dad and other dads I know? How will I navigate my fatherhood odyssey, and make history as a grateful dad?

  > *18th & Early 19th Centuries*   *Moral Overseer*
  > *Early 19th to Mid-20th Centuries*   *Distant Breadwinner*
  > *Post WWII to Mid-1960s*   *Sex Role Model*
  > *1970s / 1980s / 1990s*   *The New Father*
  > *2001 & Beyond*   *Dawn of the Grateful Dad*

Month Nine: *Gratitude Journal*

Grateful Dad: *What's new, what I notice, what I'm grateful for this month*

_____

_____

_____

_____

_____

_____

Grateful Baby: *What's new, what baby can do, what I'm grateful for with my baby this month*

_____

_____

_____

_____

_____

_____

Grateful Mom: *How are we doing? What can I do for, what I'm grateful to and for my wife/partner this month*

_____

_____

_____

_____

_____

_____

Fatherhood: *The Tenth Month*

The Ultimate Discovery

Like striking gold or finding a cure for disease, the tenth month of fatherhood may bring another amazing discovery as your baby begins to make decipherable sounds like "ma-ma" and "da-da." As one grateful dad exclaimed to me: "I swear she said my name! Really — my daughter called me *daddy*..." The start of infant language development represents the ultimate journey of discovery for babies and their parents.

Other discoveries at this time, such as figuring out how to get your baby to sleep through the night, may be equally exciting. At ten months, many new families are also discovering how to plan and pull off some weekend travel getaways to see special people or do favorite things. In these months where words emerge, and before most babies begin to walk, you will have opportunities to discover with gratitude the many magic moments that make up fatherhood.

If you are still not active in feeding your baby, make an effort to discover what, when, where, and how he likes to eat, and get involved with meals whenever possible. At ten months, most babies have expanded their culinary repertoire and you'll have fun — and get messy — when you join the mealtime feast.

New grateful dads often report one more surprising discovery by this time, as they begin to recognize the personal legacy of the man they have become. First-time fathers will notice how much they are similar to their own fathers, even noticing themselves using the same words and phrases, and behaving in ways much as their own dad did. This is a good time to do some focused, personal reflection on your own father, asking yourself questions such as:

- *When you think of your father, what comes to mind?*
- *Where was your father when you were born, and what was your father's role and level of involvement in your early years?*
- *What lessons about parenting did you learn from your father? What were the messages about fathering that showed up in his behavior? How did he role-model fatherhood?*
- *As a parent, how are you similar to and different from your father? In what ways would you like to emulate your father as a parent? How will you be a different father than your dad was?*

For some men, recalling our own fathers can be difficult. It is also almost always enlightening. Since we each have a father, we can let him be our first — and possibly our best — teacher about the ways of being a grateful dad. Whether we knew him or not, and even if we have many reasons to parent differently than he did, our own father can inform the dad we want to be. Treat this as a gift, taking the best your father gave you and pledging to be different when that makes sense instead.

First-time fathers notice how similar they are to their own fathers.

As you look toward the end of your first year of fatherhood, be assured that even greater delight awaits you.

• •

KNOW THIS:

- **Standing.** At this age babies begin to pull themselves up on furniture. They focus on this new skill that gives them a different view on the world, and they seem very much aware that standing and walking are a "big deal."

- **Help standing.** You can set up an environment that encourages standing and walking. Arrange chairs in a row or make the couch accessible to him. A few toys on the chairs might encourage him to move from one to another. Once standing, your child will learn through trial and error how to sit down. In the process of learning to stand, sit down, and walk, there will be falls; make sure sharp corners and edges are padded.

- **Standing-to-Walking.** Going from standing to walking will take four or five months of practice. Offer help and encouragement; you don't need to push. A child's own desire to learn this new way of exploring the world will be enough motivation.

TRY THIS:

- **Am I becoming my father?** Whether we know it or like it, every man grows up to resemble his own father in certain ways. We hear his voice come from our mouth, and notice in our posture, gait, and expressions that we carry our fathers around in our own bodies. Take a few minutes to reflect on these questions:

  > *When you think of your father, what comes to mind?*

  > *Where was your father when you were born, and what was your father's role and level of involvement in your early years?*

  > *What lessons about parenting did you learn from your father? What were the messages about fathering that showed up in his behavior? How did he role-model fatherhood?*

  > *As a parent, how are you similar to and different from your father? In what ways would you like to emulate your father as a parent? How will you be a different father than your dad was?*

REMEMBER THIS:

- **Calming Baby.** If you are still trying to discover how to calm your baby, remember the father-tested Boot Camp for New Dads checklist:

  > *Hungry — First, determine the last time your baby ate and if she's hungry, make sure she eats. Even if it's not her regular mealtime, a current growth spurt may suggest immediate feeding.*

  > *Gas — Next, check to see if baby may have some gas after her last meal. A burp may be all she needs to bring comfort and curtail crying.*

Or try bicycling her legs to promote relief.

> *Tired — If you're past gas, her crying may be due to baby being over-tired. Getting baby to sleep is the key task and will require a lot of finesse at this point.*

> *Diaper — One more obvious item to check is baby's diaper, which could be full or might be causing irritation. Even if it was changed recently, her diaper may be filled again.*

> *Unique — You know your baby best, so pay attention and try all of your favorite moves.*

> *Keep Trying — Repeat this checklist a few times; if you become frustrated, call on mom or someone else to take over. If you're solo, it's fine to put baby in a safe location (such as her car seat, crib, or playpen) and catch your breath for a few minutes.*

Month Ten: *Gratitude Journal*

Grateful Dad: *What's new, what I notice, what I'm grateful for this month*

_____

_____

_____

_____

_____

_____

Grateful Baby: *What's new, what baby can do, what I'm grateful for with my baby this month*

_____

_____

_____

_____

_____

_____

Grateful Mom: *How are we doing? What can I do for, what I'm grateful to and for my wife/partner this month*

_____

_____

_____

_____

_____

_____

Fatherhood: *The Eleventh Month*

Dad's Beginning to See 'Delight'

Delight becomes your experience as a father and grateful dad at eleven months, as you begin to realize that you cannot really recall life without your child. You revel in the many activities and decisions that define your family life, and you watch in continued amazement as your baby grows and becomes more verbal and more mobile.

Take a few moments to reflect on all that delights you about fatherhood and to appreciate all of the changes you have made and the challenges you've met over the last eleven months.

Now consider the many delights still to come, both in the life of your child — such as walking, talking, playing, and learning — and with your partner — including renewed levels of intimacy, more familiar sexuality, and a return to favorite activities and to a more active social life as a couple.

You begin to realize that you cannot really recall life without your child.

"My wife and I have begun to get reacquainted as a couple," says Jeff, a grateful dad. "It's as if when our baby started to talk, he reintroduced Jenny and me, and now we are dating again, kind of like when we first met."

At this delightful point in parenthood, you are poised to move forward, taking steps in your relationship to ensure its strength in the months and years ahead. "Remember your primary relationship," as my friend Dr. Michael Arloski, a psychologist and life coach, told my wife and me as new parents. He reminded us that we were together long before our son was born, and assumed that we intended to remain a couple long after our child was grown. To do so, Michael said, would require us to find a balance between being parents and being partners. This advice reminds new fathers that nurturing your partner is as critical as the love and attention you give your baby.

Grateful dads find that a simple strategy to help you *remember your primary relationship* is to create a regular date night and spend time together with your spouse doing what you enjoy most as a couple. Your time spent seeing a movie, engaged in recreation, going out with friends, or staying home alone is as essential to your family as the time you invest in being with your child. Certainly this time depends on having a trusted caregiver, whether it's a paid babysitter, a family member, or friends with whom you trade childcare. If your current list of options in this area is short, start now to brainstorm and identify who might be willing and able to provide safe, satisfactory care so that you and mom can have this important time together. You'll both be grateful for having made the effort to make the time.

At this time, it's also important to feel and express gratitude, and to be sure to share your thoughts, feelings, and reflections with your spouse. Let her know how much you appreciate all the things she does as a new mother and as your partner. Tell her also what you want and need, in order to bring greater delight to your relationship.

New grateful dads often discuss how their sex life changes with the birth of a child. By eleven months they expect a return to normalcy. As I have noted over the many months of tracing your 'daddy steps,' the delights are different than before your baby arrived. Ask yourself, "What are realistic expectations about sex at this time?" and discuss with your spouse the question "How will we approach the topic of intimacy as a couple, and how can we grow together at this time in our relationship?"

As you have already discovered, parenting is truly a delight, and one that you will continue to enjoy as the first year nears completion.

KNOW THIS:

- **Competence.** The following suggestions might help you maintain a sense of competence and a balance in your life.

  > *Know Your Child — How do you know if you are doing things right? Look to your baby for cues. If he is relaxed, responding predictably, and attentive, you are doing things right. If he cries, is unable to calm himself, does not look at you, or holds his arms and legs stiffly, he might be overwhelmed, and you need to do things differently.*

  > *Avoid Comparisons — Respect your child's unique interests, needs, and developmental timetable.*

  > *Turn to Family and Friends — Parenting can be less stressful if you seek support from family and friends. If your family does not live nearby, create an extended family. Connect with other parents you meet at work, day care, where you worship, or at parenting classes.*

  > *Rely on Your Intuition and Knowledge — To some extent you can rely on your intuition, but you also need some knowledge about how children grow and develop. Learn about your child's physical and emotional development by reading, observing your child, asking your pediatrician, and attending parenting classes.*

  > *Decide Whose Advice to Follow — When you are given conflicting advice, decide whose advice matches your values and your child.*

  > *Celebrate Your Successes — Recognize your successes and enjoy them.*

  > *Enjoy Time with Your Child — Find things that you both like to do together.*

  > *Take Care of Yourself — Keep yourself physically fit, well nourished, and well rested. Adjusting to a new baby is physically and emotionally demanding. Fatigue can make coping more difficult and lead a grateful dad to question his parenting skills, especially when things are not going well.*

TRY THIS:

- **Got Questions?** When the going gets good, grateful dads ask and reflect on questions like these:

  > *What has changed and challenged me most as a new grateful dad?*

  > *What delights are still to come as a father?*

  > *What am I most grateful for, and to whom am I most grateful, as a new dad?*

  > *What are realistic expectations about sex with my partner at this time?*

  > *How will we approach the topic of intimacy as a couple, and how can we grow together at this time in our relationship?*

REMEMBER THIS:

- **Your Primary Relationship.** You and mom were together before your baby was born, and you can assume that you'll remain a couple long after your child is grown. Healthy, long-term relationships take work, just as you are working hard to be a truly active, grateful dad. Some suggestions for keeping the love alive:

  > *Find a balance between being parents and partners — Blind focus on baby takes a toll on your primary relationship. Work on being a couple.*

  > *Set a regular date night and spend time together doing what you enjoy most as a couple — Catch a movie, play and recreate, see friends, stay home. Doing what you love, together as a couple, is as essential to your family as the time you invest in being with your child.*

  > *Express gratitude to those who make your life rich and full — Consider how much you have to be grateful for in the mother of your child. Share your thoughts, feelings, and reflections with her. Let her know how much you appreciate all the things she does as a new mother and as your partner. Do this with other important people who contributed to you being a grateful dad.*

  > *Express your needs — Tell your partner what you want and need in order to bring greater delight to your relationship.*

Month Eleven: *Gratitude Journal*

Grateful Dad: *What's new, what I notice, what I'm grateful for this month*

Grateful Baby: *What's new, what baby can do, what I'm grateful for with my baby this month*

Grateful Mom: *How are we doing? What can I do for, what I'm grateful to and for my wife/partner this month*

Fatherhood: *The Twelfth Month*

Delight Shines

Hooray! Here you are, a Grateful Dad for one entire year. As you prepare to celebrate your child's first birthday, be sure to include a celebration of yourself and your partner to commemorate the grateful dad and mom you have become. Both of you have experienced and thrived in the face of many profound changes. As you've witnessed and enriched your baby's growth and development over the first year of life, your own lives — as parents and as people — have been enhanced in ways you never imagined. So, just as your child has reached an important milestone, her father and mother are also arriving at a monumental new place in their own lives.

At this notable juncture, I want to pause and say *thank you* for permitting me to offer some thoughts, suggestions, and experiences that I hope were of some value during the first year of fatherhood. I am grateful to all who've taken the time to read this. I have actually imagined grateful dads (and grateful moms) reading this little book as they held their little baby and climbed together up the 'daddy steps.' From the early days of *delivery*, and the difficult climb through *deprivation*, I pictured you all learning and growing together as a family. And as the light of *discovery* gave way more recently to the rewards of *delight*, my vision joins yours in looking toward the many happy, healthy years ahead. I am grateful that you've taken the time to read and consider these ideas, each step of the way.

As you know, every family in America has the opportunity to find a meaningful and satisfying lifestyle. The challenge of balancing work and family demands is at once universal in our society and unique for each couple.

It's seldom easy to do, as no simple road map exists to point the way, and whatever route we choose comes with advantages and drawbacks. Whether one of you stays home, or both go back to work, is something only you can decide. Yet it should help to remember that you are not alone; indeed, new families everywhere are facing similar decisions and asking these same, difficult questions. Remember that many resources exist, and seek out the people who can best support you along the way.

Father and mother are arriving at a monumental new place in their lives.

As a new grateful dad, you know that your greatest contribution as a man is to prepare your child to find their way in the world. While it may seem an awesome and daunting task, it becomes more manageable when taken one year at a time. Dr. Bruce Linton, a family counselor and founder of the Fathers' Forum, suggests that each grateful dad should pause annually, on or around their child's birthday, and consider the following questions:

· *What kind of father does my child need this year?*
· *What particular experiences will my child be having this year?*
· *What particular involvement and support does my child need from me this year?*
· *What support does my child already receive from others (e.g.-mom, teachers, etc.)?*
· *As a man, what is it that I may offer that is unique, that my child is not receiving elsewhere?*

By answering these questions, you will have a good idea of what you can do to be the best possible father to your child.

In this time of delight, as you look back through the haze of this amazing year and ahead to many, many years of joy, be assured that much of the uncertainty of fatherhood will become a bit easier, and that, as you found during this first year, being a grateful dad just keeps getting better all the time.

. . . .

KNOW THIS:

- **Setting Limits.** In the process of becoming independent, your child will explore, touch, and examine everything. She should not be allowed to do whatever she wants, but the way in which she is disciplined is important to her later development. Teaching limits within a safe environment, and in a way that allows her to develop a healthy sense of independence, requires both kindness and firmness.

- **Right and Wrong.** By setting limits, you will be teaching your child right from wrong, self-control, and respect for the rights and feelings of others. In addition you will be protecting your child from harm. Though you begin to set limits and teach these ideas now, it will be a long time before your child fully understands these ideas.

TRY THIS:

- **Discipline Dos & Don'ts.** As you begin to discipline your child, keep the following in mind:

  > Though discipline is often thought of as rules and punishment, it actually means to teach, to lead, to guide, and to train.

  > At this age, your child does not understand the meaning of the word "no." He will gradually learn that it means "No, not right now." Next he will need to learn that it might also mean "never."

  > Set up your child's environment so there are as few "no"s as possible. Put away your belongings that might get damaged; put barriers in front of things that need to be off limits.

  > Make your list of what is off limits as short as possible. Too many "no"s can overwhelm a young child and make it harder for her to learn what is okay and what is not okay.

  > Consistency is important. Say "no" to those things that are really important to you, so that you will always follow through. Rules become

meaningless if you allow your child to do something one day and don't allow it the next.

> *If your first "no" is ineffective, it is important to follow through with action. Redirect your child's attention to another toy; offer something else to do; remove him from the scene; explain in simple words why certain things are not okay.*

REMEMBER THIS:

• **Ask Annually.** While it may seem an awesome and daunting task, fatherhood becomes more manageable when taken one year at a time. Dr. Bruce Linton, a family counselor and founder of the Fathers' Forum, suggests that each grateful dad should pause annually, on or around their child's birthday, and consider these questions:

> *What kind of father does my child need this year?*

> *What particular experiences will my child be having this year?*

> *What particular involvement and support does my child need from me this year?*

> *What support does my child already receive from others (e.g.-mom, teachers, etc.)?*

> *As a man, what is it that I may offer that is unique, that my child is not receiving elsewhere?*

Month Twelve: *Gratitude Journal*

Grateful Dad: *What's new, what I notice, what I'm grateful for this month*

_____

_____

_____

_____

_____

_____

Grateful Baby: *What's new, what baby can do, what I'm grateful for with my baby this month*

_____

_____

_____

_____

_____

_____

Grateful Mom: *How are we doing? What can I do for, what I'm grateful to and for my wife/partner this month*

_____

_____

_____

_____

_____

_____

About the Author

Doug Gertner is The Grateful Dad. He is Marc Gertner's son, partner to Maggie Miller, father of a teen-ager, Jordy Gertner, and an educator, speaker, broadcaster, author, and activist who brings a laid-back, rock-n-roll wisdom to the topic of dads and dudes, including his engaging stories, top tips, quick quips, skills, ideas, exercises, and activities to reflect on our own dads and bring father-friendliness to every situation. Doug and his family make their home in Denver, Colorado, and as The Grateful Dad his 'long, strange trip' takes Doug far and wide teaching, training, and speaking about the joys and challenges for fathers and families.

His professional career includes service to higher education, non-profit, small business, corporate, and independent consulting. He has consulted for the Colorado Foundation for Families and Children, the Colorado Fatherhood Connection, Boot Camp for New Dads, The New Fathers Foundation, Family Star Montessori Early Head Start, Mile High Montessori Head Start, Families First of Augusta (Maine), Catholic Charities Head Start, Colorado Family Support Council, Celebrate Family Festival, Creative Options Early Learning Center, Denver Jewish Community Center Early Childhood Center, Mile High United Way, State of Colorado, Adams, Chaffee, El Paso, Fremont, Jefferson, Montrose, Pueblo and Weld Counties (Colorado), inJoy Videos, and Policy Studies Inc. Doug is a member of the National Training Team of Boot Camp for New Dads.

Doug earned his doctorate from the College of Education, Division of Professional Psychology, at University of Northern Colorado, his masters degree from Teachers College, Columbia University, and his bachelors degree from Kenyon College. He has taught at ten colleges and universities in Colorado and Wyoming, lectured, published, and consulted widely in the area of gender studies. He is a member of the Leadership Collective of the National Organization for Men Against Sexism, co-chair of the Men's Studies Association, and was an Associate Editor of the journal *Men and Masculinities.*

Doug has completed professional development in mediation and conflict resolution, advanced interpersonal communication, diversity and intercultural communication, personal/professional coaching, and experiential and accelerated learning. He is an avid telemark skier, enjoys mountain biking, live music, and cheering for Denver sports teams.

Top Keynote Speech & Workshop Topics for The Grateful Dad include:

· The Grateful Dad's Guide to a Modern Fatherhood Odyssey: Debunking the Myths of Historical Father Figures
· The Grateful Dad: How to Be (or Support) a Truly Involved Father
· GLAD to be a DAD: Gratitude and Fatherhood
· Field of Dads: Creating a Father-Friendly Environment
· Fathers Matter: Why and How to Keep Dad in the Loop
· Playtime for Pops: A Playshop for Fun-Loving Fathers
· Daddy Balance = Family Balance - A Life Planning Workshop for Anyone Who Wants It ALL!
· Power Tools for Parenting: A Program for Dads to Inspire Passion, Joy, & Gratitude in Fatherhood

For more information about how to bring on The Grateful Dad, contact:
Doug Gertner, Ph.D. / The Grateful Dad
7949 East 28th Place, Denver, CO 80238
303.377.8081 · 303.886.4114
doug@thegratefuldad.org · www.thegratefuldad.org

The Grateful Dad Shop

The Grateful Dad's Journal of Gratitude: A Daily Place to Celebrate Your Life

When you make it a habit to be grateful, you realize just how much is going right in your life. A daily practice with gratitude brings more good stuff your way every day. *The Grateful Dad's Journal of Gratitude* is A Daily Place to Celebrate Your Life. Get one or more and just go for it. Includes helpful hints, inspiring quotes, and plenty of room to note what you're thankful for and expand on the gifts that you get every day. (72 pages; softcover with spiral binding for easy use with daily entries.)
$12.50 each, postage paid / 2 for $20.00 /5 for $35.00 (includes Shipping & Handling).

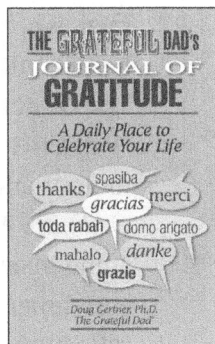

The Official Grateful Dad T-Shirt

Are you a grateful dad, or do you know one? The Grateful Dad now has an all-new Official Grateful Dad T-shirt and we want you to be the first guy on your block to wear one, so we'll send you this great new design for just $20.00. Trippy blue text, on a manly black heavy cotton T, this is the perfect gift for every grateful dad you know.
Sizes: MED / LG / XL / XXL. $20.00 (includes Shipping & Handling).

Men's Anthology

Every man has a story, and now, there's a book that tells those stories. *Ordinary Men, Extraordinary Lives: Defining Moments* tells the first person, authentic, life-altering experiences of 40 soulful men, who courageously share their hearts, guts, and psyches. Doug Gertner, The Grateful Dad, contributed his essay "Full Circle Fatherhood, or How I lost my mother and became The Grateful Dad." Order your copy of *Ordinary Men, Extraordinary Lives* and enjoy the enlightening insights. Gift it to a man or woman who is seeking enrichment, or anyone who appreciates deep sharing and reflection.

$15.00 (includes Shipping & Handling).

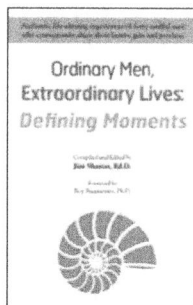

The Grateful Dad's Guide to the First Year of Fatherhood: How to Parent Your Newborn with Passion, Joy & Gratitude

Get more copies of this go-to guide with hands-on month-by-month advice, tools, and strategies for every grateful dad. $15.00 (includes Shipping & Handling).

To order any of these products, go to The Grateful Dad Shop: www.thegratefuldad.org/shop.

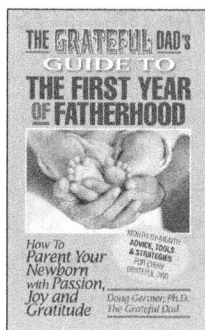

The New Grateful Dads Group
Real-Time Coaching for Real New Dads

HEY NEW DADS:
Are You a Grateful Dad or Do You Want To Be One?

- Would you like a way to talk with other new dads about this new gig?
- Are you wondering how to keep the love alive (or re-spark it) with mom?
- Do you want expert advice on how to be the best possible father, today?
- Do you worry about how your father may influence the way you are as a dad?
- Are you ready to show your commitment to being an involved new father?
- Do you realize that the advice of other dads is some of the best you'll find?
- Would you like monthly accountability and ideas to keep you focused, on track, and energized as a new father?

If YOUR ANSWER is YES! then
THE NEW GRATEFUL DADS GROUP is for YOU!

THE NEW GRATEFUL DADS GROUP is your fast track path to transforming your life to become a truly grateful dad.

The New Grateful Dads Group is an intentional community of involved, committed fathers who dedicate time daily, weekly, and monthly to being grateful dads, together and independently, with appreciation for the many rewards and benefits it brings to themselves, their child, and their partner. Specially designed by Doug Gertner, Ph.D., The Grateful Dad®, The New Grateful Dads Group is a monthly mastermind group coaching experience, meeting virtually, to learn and support the rewards of being a fully involved father, and help you get more out of every day, and enhance your relationship and communication with your wife or partner. Doug has personally experienced and harnessed the power of being a grateful dad, and he can help you take the 'daddy steps' to do the same.

Registration for THE NEW GRATEFUL DADS GROUP gets you:

- **Monthly Mastermind Group Coaching Sessions** — 90 minutes each
- **"Dad Download" during every meeting** — time focused just on you
- **Bonus Content** — learn something new about fatherhood every month
- **Optional One-on-One Meetings with Doug** — between sessions
- **On-Call Access to Doug Gertner, The Grateful Dad** — here if you need me
- **Private FACEBOOK Group** — access to your own on-line community
- **The Official Grateful Dad T-shirt** — wear it proud!
- **The Grateful Dad's Guide to the First Year of Fatherhood: How To Parent Your Newborn with Passion, Joy & Gratitude** — Free book, free e-book, & free audio book
- **BONUS: The Grateful Dad's Journal of Gratitude** — sign up for a full year package and get a one year supply of this popular gratitude journal too

A $6,163 value, offered at rock-bottom introductory pricing now!

MORE DETAILS about *The New Grateful Dads Group*

· The New Grateful Dads Group Fatherhood Mastermind meets together in a conference call or on-line session for 1-2 hours of intensive learning and celebration on dates TBD.

· Every session includes a check-in by each member with their current 'daddy steps' update, an extended deep dive into fatherhood content, plus a "Dad Download" — solo attention to each new father's current needs, challenges, and celebrations.

· Members also have the option to receive one-on-one fatherhood coaching conversations with Doug Gertner, The Grateful Dad®, plus access to their own Facebook group, and free copies of *The Grateful Dad's Guide to the First Year of Fatherhood: How To Parent Your Newborn with Passion, Joy & Gratitude*, as a free book, free e-book, and free audio book.

· The New Grateful Dads Group is a simple, ready-to-use way of accessing all of the rewards and benefits that come from being a truly involved and grateful dad.

SPACE is LIMITED! Join today so you don't miss out.

Register @
www.thegratefuldad.org/thenewgratefuldadsgroup/
For more info, contact Doug Gertner:
doug@thegratefuldad.org

THE GRATEFUL DAD®

Praise for
The Grateful Dad's Guide to The First Year of Fatherhood

"I have been a grateful dad for over 30 years. I just wish I had met Doug when I was first starting out as a father. Who better than Doug Gertner, THE Grateful Dad himself, to help new fathers as they begin their journey of discovery and challenges that will guide them in the most important job they'll ever undertake. Doug provides great information in an easy to read format that will help new and seasoned fathers have the confidence to step up to the plate. This is a book that will be much used at the Center on Fathering and one that I hope every father reads."
Ken Sanders, Director and Founder
Center on Fathering of Colorado Springs
Colorado

"I love the holistic approach of the book, its honesty about the challenges, and the practical solutions that are offered. It's very user-friendly for a busy new dad, a fun read, and a helpful companion with each changing month of growth, discovery, and confusion. Being a new dad is a steep learning curve. I like that the book doesn't pretend that it won't be, but gives you places to rest along the way, and lets you know that you're not alone in this."
Ryan Jaret
New Dad
Maine

Made in the USA
Monee, IL
22 March 2025

14395266R00046